Paintings and Ponderings

January to June, 2020

Darleen Armstrong

Copyright © 2020 Darleen Armstrong

All rights reserved.
No part of this book may be reproduced or published in any manner without written permission of the copyright owner except for the use of quotations in a book review.
For more information please feel free to contact
LoveBecauseJesusLoves@gmail.com.

First Edition
Paperback ISBN: 9798622837540
Independently published

Cover art and all acrylic paintings by Darleen Armstrong

Unless otherwise indicated, all Scripture quotations are from The ESV® Bible (The Holy Bible, English Standard Version®), copyright © 2001 by Crossway, a publishing ministry of Good News Publishers. Used by permission. All rights reserved.

Scripture quotations marked (NLT) are taken from the Holy Bible, New Living Translation, copyright © 1996, 2004, 2007, 2013, 2015 by Tyndale House Foundation. Used by permission of Tyndale House Publishers, Inc., Carol Stream, Illinois 60188. All rights reserved.

Grace to you and peace from God our
Father and the Lord Jesus Christ.
I thank my God in all my remembrance of you, always
in every prayer of mine for you all making my prayer
with joy, because of your partnership in the gospel from
the first day until now. And I am sure of this, that He
who began a good work in you will bring it to
completion at the day of Jesus Christ.

Philippians 1:2-6

Acknowledgments:

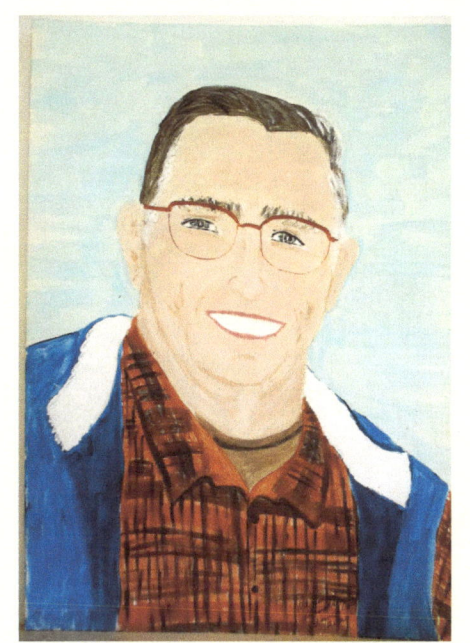

The first half of 2020 was unusual and eventful for just about everyone across our nation and even around the world. The impact of the corona virus pandemic has varied greatly. I know that many have struggled and suffered. The months of sheltering at home allowed me more time for Bible reading and reflection. Another blessing came through Debi Criss, a delightful, creative and loving woman from our church who led online weekly paint nights. She wanted to provide creative fun and opportunity for women to connect while physically isolated. Thanks so much Debi for sharing yourself and your talent so generously! You provided models for most of these paintings.

I also want to thank my family. My hubby Randy has encouraged me for years to take more time for art, buying supplies for me as hints every so often. Hon, thanks even more for increasing my love for the Lord and His Word as you have shared insights from your Bible studies. Our twin daughters are great cheerleaders and can be counted on to gush with appreciation for each of my efforts. Rachel, your comments have meant a lot, especially as you surpass me in talent. Your drawn and painted animals are full of life! Anita, besides your encouraging responses to specific paintings, thank you for the many hours you spent on layout, coaxing your computer to display each page, with script and images, according to your high standards. Thanks also to our special Stephanie who provided giggles and laughter as background music while I painted.

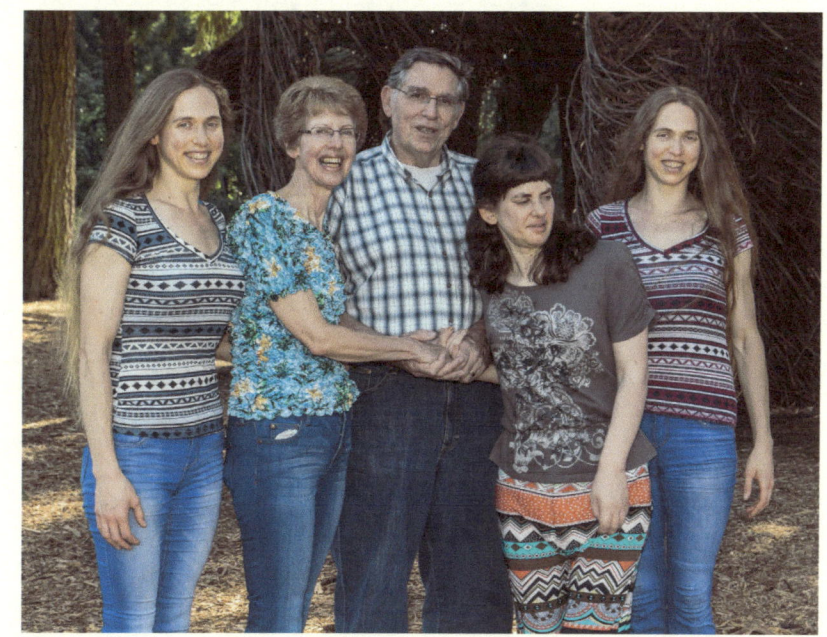

Most of all, thank You Lord Jesus for revealing a little more of Yourself, Your perspective and Your love to me over these last months. You are the Supreme Artist, displaying ever-changing beauty in your creation all around us. Thank you for giving us opportunity and joy in using Your gifts of creativity.

The paintings were not originally intended as illustrations. However, I found each one brought truths to mind that have blessed me recently. So I pray that these humble paintings and ponderings may bless you in some way.

Darleen

By this you know the Spirit of God: every spirit that confesses that Jesus Christ has come in the flesh is from God, and every spirit that does not confess Jesus is not from God. Beloved, let us love one another, for love is from God, and whoever loves has been born of God and knows God. Anyone who does not love does not know God, because God is love. In this is the love of God was made manifest among us, that God sent His Only Son into the world, so that we might live through Him. In this is love, not that we have loved God but that He loved us and sent His Son to be the propitiation for our sins.

1 John 4:2–3, 7–10

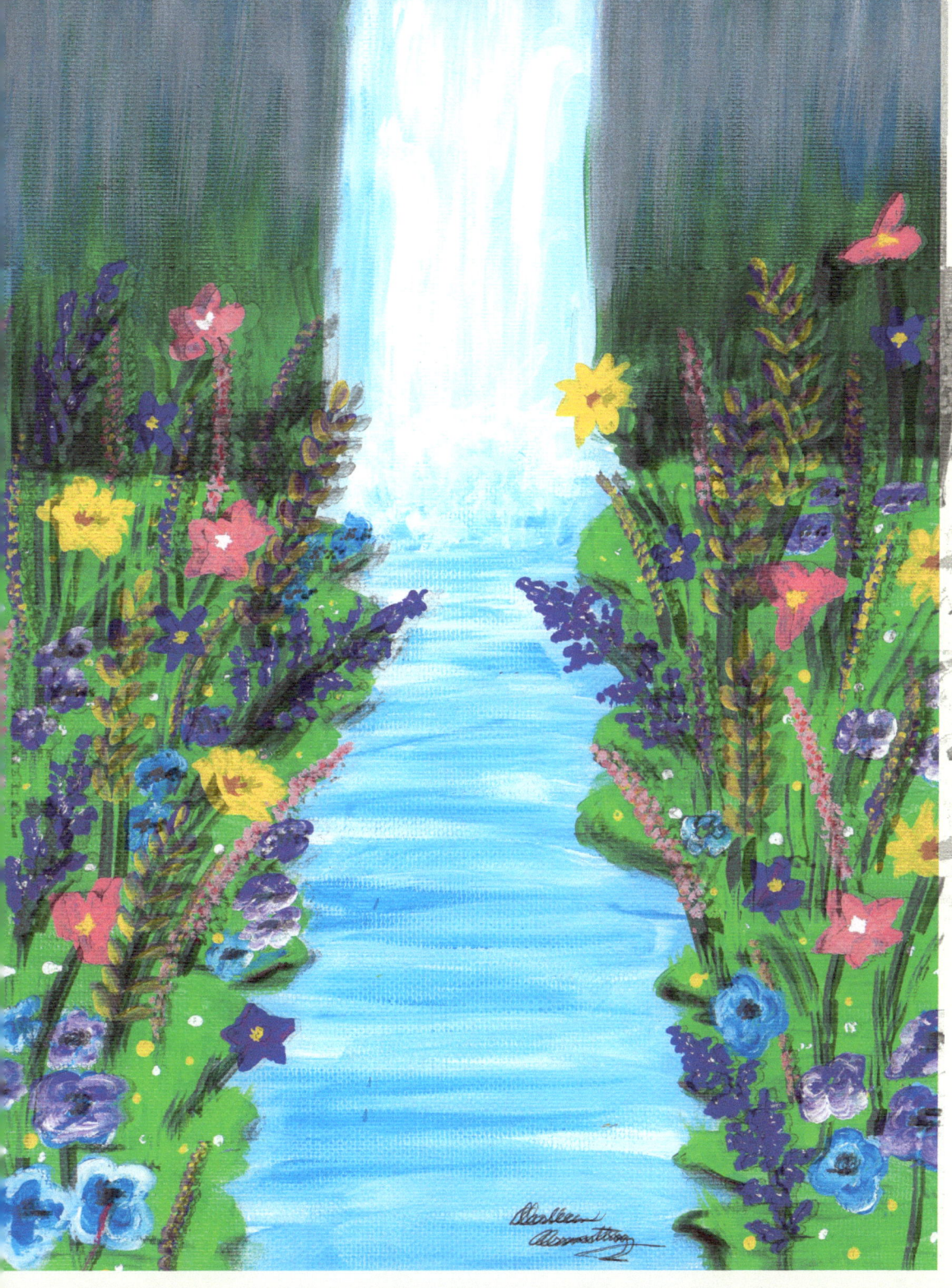

"But the fruit of the Spirit is love, joy, peace, patience, kindness, goodness, faithfulness, gentleness, self-control; against such things there is no law. And those who belong to Christ Jesus have crucified the flesh with its passions and desires. If we live by the Spirit, let us also keep in step with the Spirit." (Gal 5:22-25 ESV)

My January focus for this year is to yield more to the Holy Spirit. Pondering this, I've found the teaching of John Randall, senior pastor of Calvary Chapel San Juan Capistrano, California, helpful. The Lord used him to remind me that the Holy Spirit primarily leads through His Word and never in opposition to it. John pointed out that our part is to read the Bible prayerfully, asking God to lead, being ready to obey. God's leading doesn't mean all will go smoothly, but the Holy Spirit does give deep assurance and peace. John helped me realize that the Holy Spirit's leading is both SUPERNATURAL and NATURAL. It isn't weird, yet often not what we expect.

"But the fruit of the Spirit is love, joy, peace, patience, kindness, goodness, faithfulness, gentleness, self-control." (Galatians 5:22-23)
The fruit of the Holy Spirit is LOVE. All the rest are aspects of love. We grow in fruitfulness as we invite and allow the Holy Spirit to control.

Help me Lord to sink roots deeply into Your Word with a readiness to obey what You direct, so that my life will bear fruit for eternity, flourishing like the flowers.

By faith Abraham obeyed when he was called to go out to a place that he was to receive as an inheritance. ...For he was looking forward to the city that has foundations, whose designer and builder is God. By faith Sarah herself received power to conceive, even when she was past the age, since she considered Him faithful who had promised. Therefore from one man, and him as good as dead, were born descendants as many as the stars of heaven and as many as the innumerable grains of sand by the seashore. These all died in faith, not having received the things promised, but having seen them and greeted them from afar, and having acknowledged that they were strangers and exiles on the earth ...they desire a better country, that is, a heavenly one. Therefore God is not ashamed to be called their God, for He has prepared for them a city.

Hebrews 11:8-16

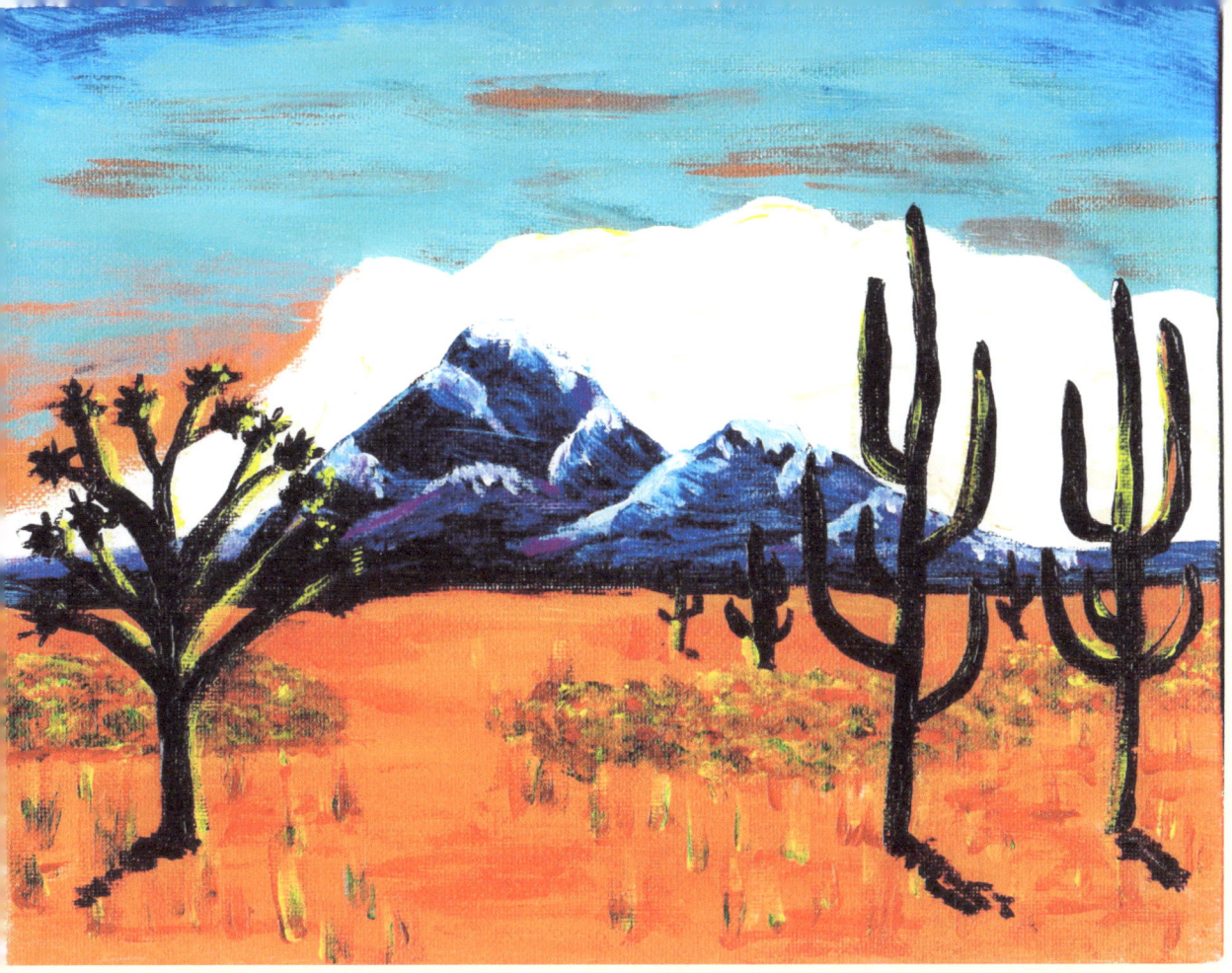

This semi-arid landscape reminds my hubby of his home state of New Mexico. Though it appears deserted and lifeless to this Wisconsin girl, many plants and animals thrive there. Plus, it promises to burst into bloom whenever there are sudden rain showers.

I've been reading Abraham and Sarah's drama recorded in Genesis 12-21. Abram (as he was first called) stands out as a man of faith who left his home land in obedience to God, traveling with his family to an uncertain place. In fact, he never owned land in the place God promised to give his descendants, living as a nomad in tents. His failings are also recorded. Twice, traveling in enemy territory, he feared for his life and told a half truth, claiming his wife Sarai as his sister. The LORD graciously protected and delivered them both times. When told as an aging man with no children that he would have descendants like the stars of the heavens, he believed God. That faith was counted to him as righteousness. *(Geneses 15:6)*

But the years dragged on and Sarai grew impatient. She thought of a way to make the promise come true. She devised a plan. She followed a common cultural practice and gave her maid, Hagar, to her husband to bear a son for her. Ouch! How often have I tried by my own ideas and effort to make something happen? Sarai's action seemed initially successful, but yielded much pain and hostility. This started in her own family and has continued through the centuries between descendants of Hagar's son Ishmael and those of Isaac, the promised child that God finally gave her at ninety years of age. Just before Isaac's conception, God renamed the couple to signify that they would be parents of a large nation of people. God, indeed, kept His promise, but His timing was not what they expected.

Help me, Heavenly Father, to trust Your presence and promises when circumstances around me look bleak. And warn me if I try and "help You" with my own efforts when Your answers seem delayed. **You can be trusted to cause all things to work together for our good and for Your glory as we respond to Your love in faith. (Romans 8:28)**

The steadfast love of the Lord never ceases; His mercies never come to an end; they are new every morning; great is Your faithfulness.
"'The Lord is my portion,' says my soul,
'therefore I will hope in Him.'"
The Lord is good to those who wait for Him,
to the soul who seeks Him.
It is good that one should wait quietly for
the salvation of the Lord.

Lamentations 3:22-26

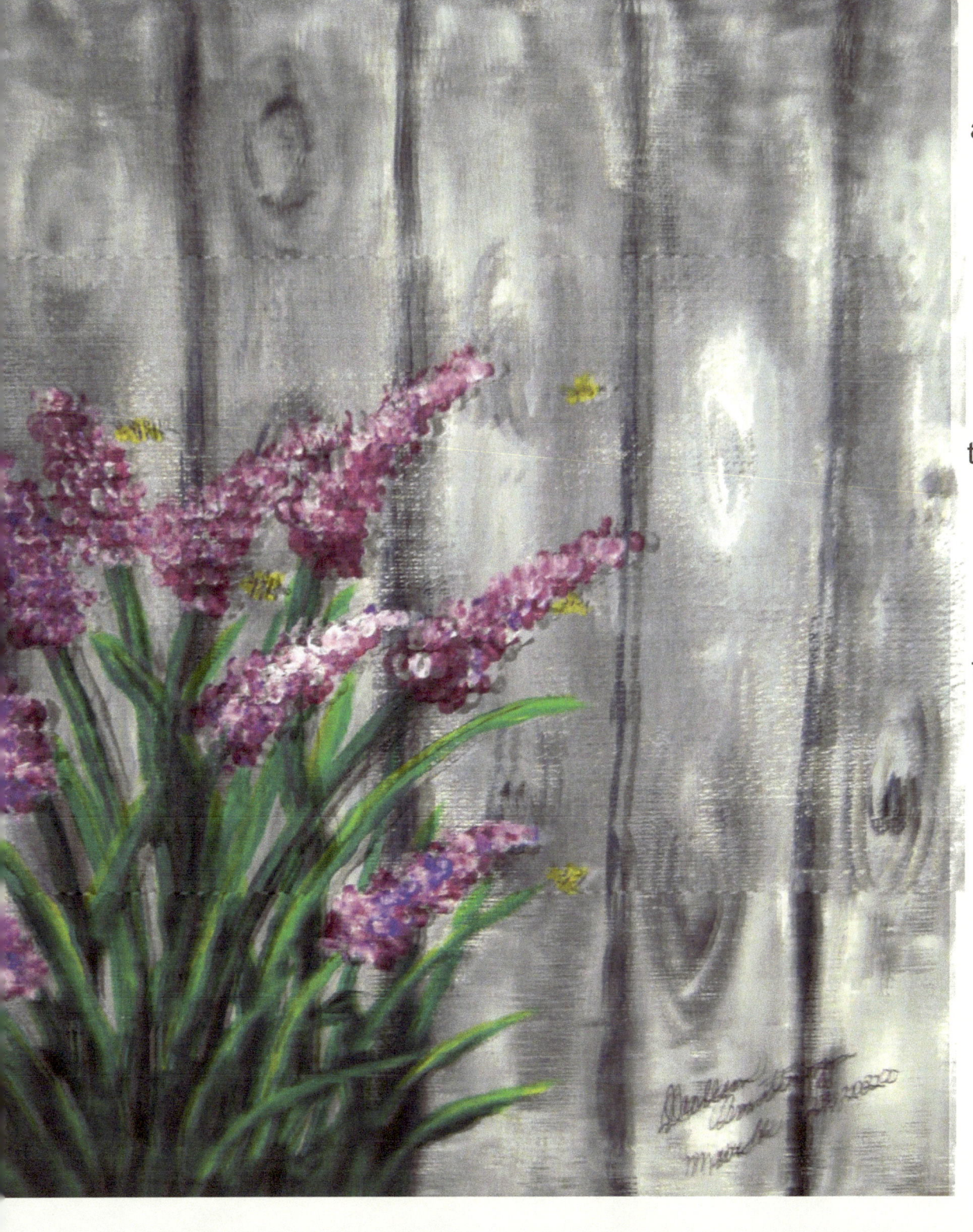

"Holiness in Hidden Places" is a delightful book written by Joni Eareckson Tada. It is a treasure, containing beautiful, original art work throughout. Joni lives as a radiant, productive, and joyful woman despite being quadriplegic since her diving accident at age 17. What a mentor and model of trusting God through difficult experiences! Thousands of individuals with all kinds of disabilities have received practical, emotional and spiritual help through her organization: Joni and Friends.

This lavender growing by an old fence illustrates her challenge to be open to God's beauty, truth and hope from unexpected places. I'm learning to live in the moment, taking time to be grateful for things like a delicate wildflower, sunlight piercing Oregon clouds, a family hiking together, or the giggles of my special daughter replaying video snippets of *Sesame Street, Caillou,* or *Mister Rogers Neighborhood* for the thousandth time on her computer. Frequently, in the Psalms we are exhorted to give thanks to the LORD. Psalm 118 begins and ends with this: *"Oh give thanks to the LORD, for He is good; for His steadfast love endures forever!"*

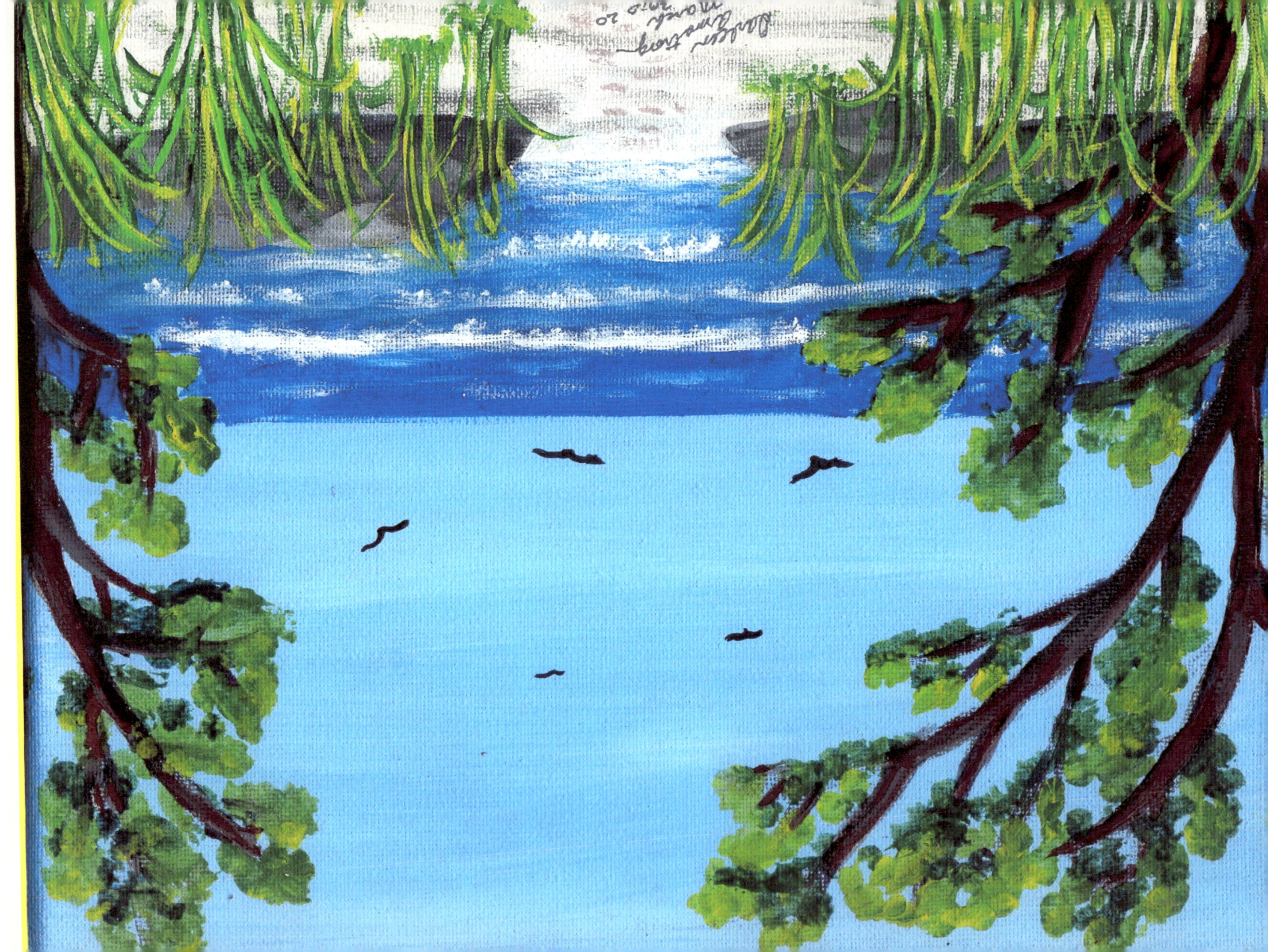

With the scare of the corona virus, schools, many businesses, gyms and even worship services have been shut down, not only across America, but even around the world. During this pandemic, we are expected to stay quarantined at home, keeping distant from others. Many friends are sewing fabric masks, since we are supposed to cover nose and mouth if we need to venture out and then are required to keep at least six feet away from anyone else. Many have lost jobs or had to close their businesses; parents have been stretched by needing to supervise their children's schooling at home; contacts, even with doctors, have become virtual; vacation plans have been postponed or canceled. We wonder when we can return to normal life?

In this painting, it's like we're viewing an inviting beach just beyond the rocks, just out of reach. May we turn our uncertainties and longings to the only One Who knows the future. In fact, He is sovereign over the present and has His purposes for all that is happening today.

Heavenly Father, I would give You my uncertainties and anxious thoughts today. Do all that You desire to do in me through this season. **"Let your reasonableness be known to everyone. The Lord is at hand; do not be anxious about anything, but in everything by prayer and supplication with thanksgiving let your requests be made known to God. And the peace of God, which surpasses all understanding, will guard your hearts and your minds in Christ Jesus."** *(Philippians 4:5-7)*

When we were utterly helpless, Jesus Christ came at just the right time and died for us sinners. Now, most people would not be willing to die for an upright person, though someone might perhaps be willing to die for a person who is especially good. But God showed His great love for us by sending Christ to die for us while we were still sinners. And since we have been made right in God's sight by the blood of Christ, He will certainly save us from God's condemnation. For since our friendship with God was restored by the death of His Son while we were still His enemies, we will certainly be saved through the life of His Son. So now we can rejoice in our wonderful new relationship with God because our Lord Jesus Christ has made us friends of God.

Romans 5:6-11 (NLT)

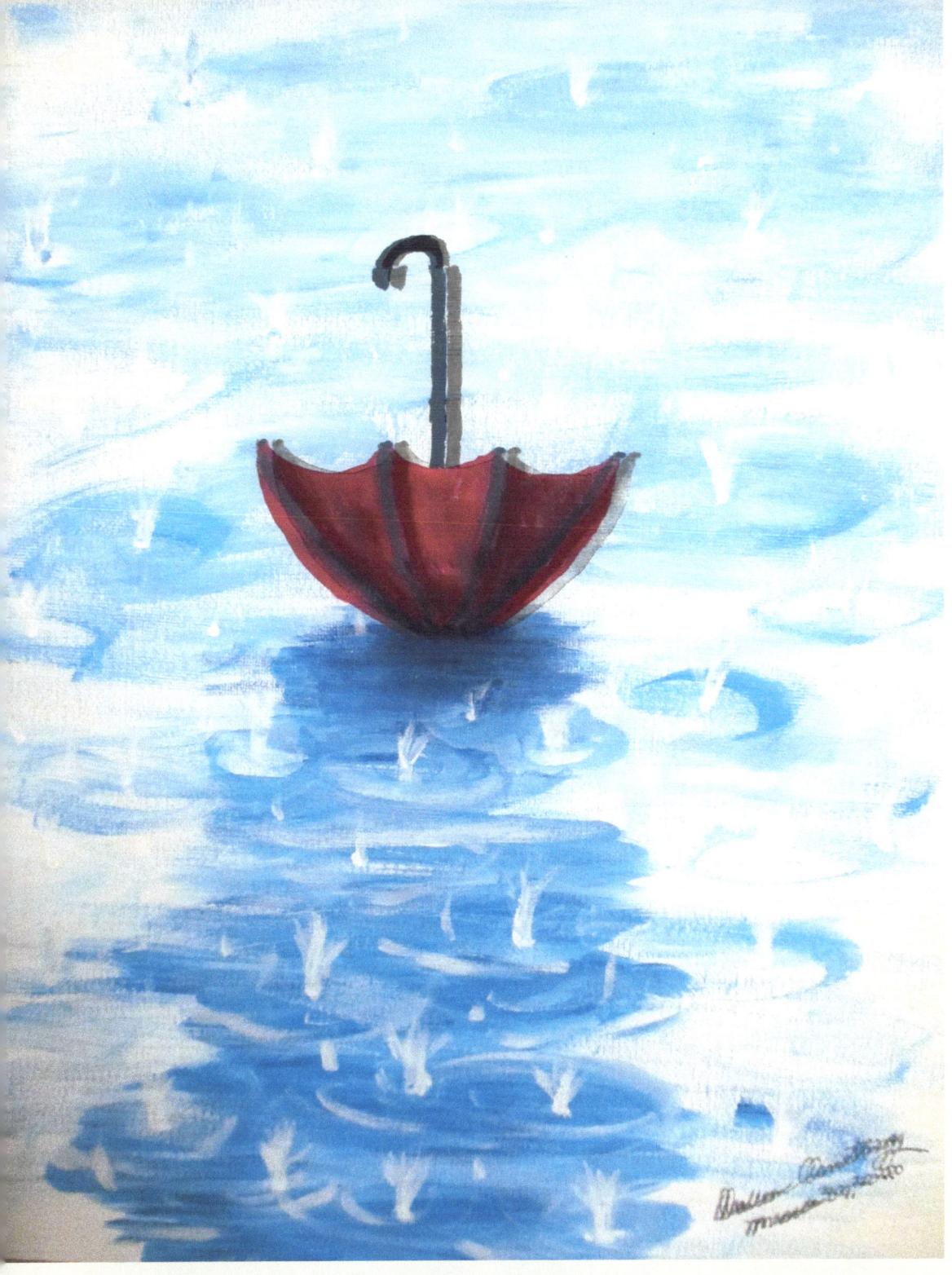

Debi Criss has been leading a weekly painting class online for whomever is interested from our Harvest Community Church fellowship during this pandemic. When she led us in painting an upside down, soaked umbrella, it matched my reading as well as our weather. We've had a series of cloudy, rainy days in Oregon.

At the same time, I've slogged through daily readings in I and II Kings, weary of how many kings of Israel and Judah "did what was evil in the sight of the LORD." There were victorious bright spots, like the sunbreaks we celebrate in the Pacific Northwest, but even the heir of a God-honoring king often turned back to idolatry.

The sinful nature of mankind is deeper and broader than I like to think. Indeed, *"all have sinned and fall short of the glory of God." (Romans 3:23)* How desperately we need a Savior! Thank You Christ Jesus for entering the mess of our sinful world to become our perfect substitute, taking God's wrath for our sin on Yourself at the cross. *"But God shows His love for us in that while we were still sinners, Christ died for us." (Romans 5:8)*

The god of this world has blinded the minds of the unbelievers, to keep them from seeing the light of the gospel of the glory of Christ, Who is the image of God. For what we proclaim is not ourselves, but Jesus Christ as Lord, with ourselves as your servants for Jesus' sake. For God, Who said, "Let light shine out of darkness," has shone in our hearts to give the light of the knowledge of the glory of God in the Face of Jesus Christ.

2 Corninthains 4:4-6

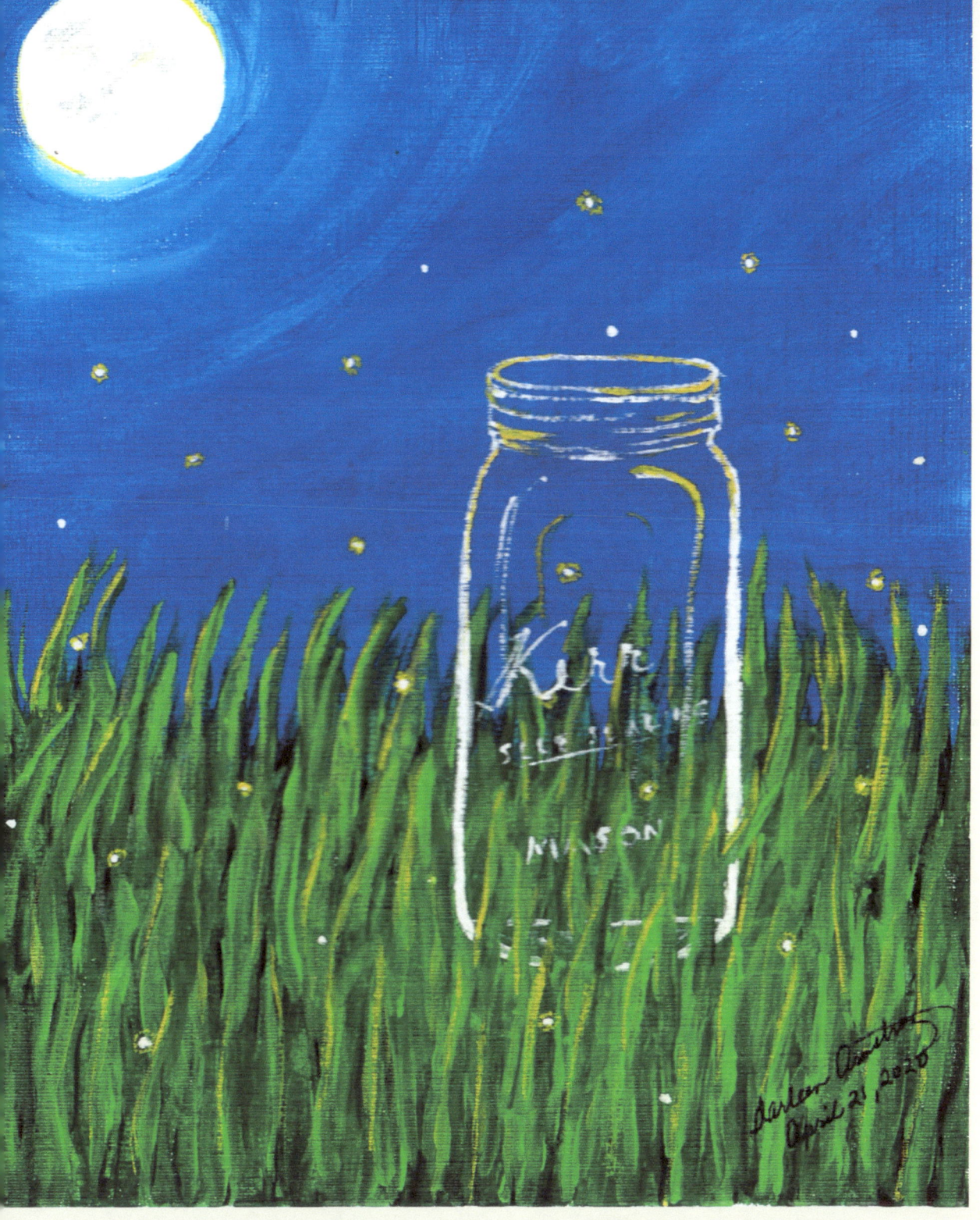

When Debi suggested that we paint fireflies, my mind took me back to the mid 1950's, visiting my eldest sister's home on Long Island, NY. I had never before experienced the magical, fairy like sparks of light that flittered around her backyard. My niece and nephews joined in the game attempting to capture a few to hold in a jar. We had some success, but couldn't stand to keep them imprisoned for long.

Sometimes this world seems so dark. Listening to newscasts can be depressing, especially with the divisiveness, hatred and violence demonstrated in rioting across our nation recently. In the Apostle John's opening statements about Jesus, he said,
"In Him was life, and the life was the light of men. The light shines in the darkness, and the darkness has not overcome it."
(John 1:4-5)

Even the tiny sparks of fireflies light up a dark night. In Jesus' longest recorded sermon or teaching, He exhorted all who believe in Him to let their lights shine.
"You are the light of the world. A city set on a hill cannot be hidden. Nor do people light a lamp and put it under a basket, but on a stand, and it gives light to all in the house. In the same way, let your light shine before others, so that they may see your good works and give glory to your Father who is in heaven."
(Matthew 5:14-16)
So let's shine like fireflies for Jesus Christ!

Rejoice in the Lord always; again I will say, rejoice. Let your reasonableness be known to everyone. The Lord is at hand; do not be anxious about anything, but in everything by prayer and supplication with thanksgiving let your requests be made known to God. And the peace of God, which surpasses all understanding, will guard your hearts and your minds in Christ Jesus.

Philippians 4:4-7

When Randy and I visited Israel a few years back, "shalom" was the one Hebrew word that I recognized and could use. "Shalom" is commonly used as a greeting when meeting or departing. But its meaning is anything but common or shallow. Shalom speaks of deep peace and well-being, of everything in harmony.

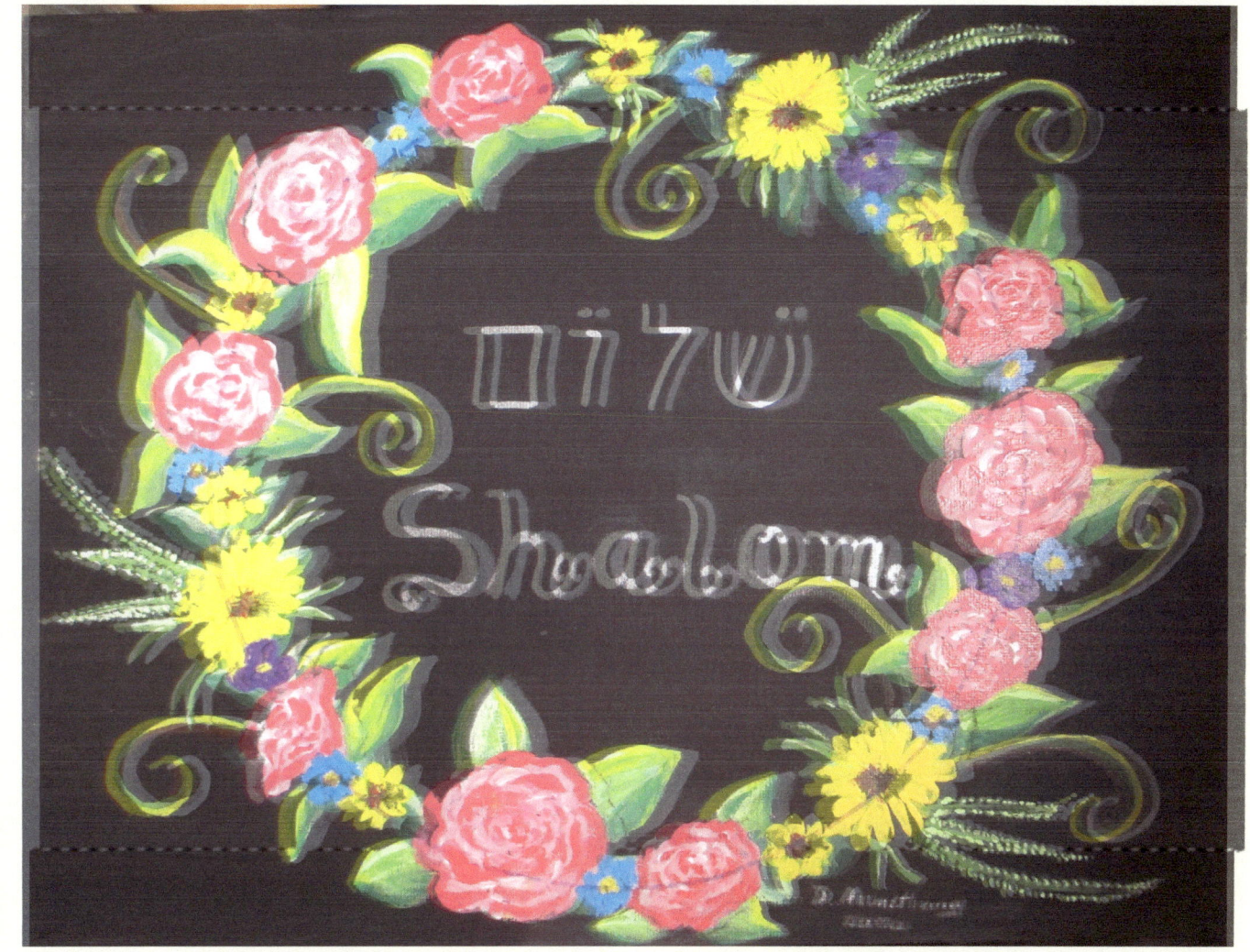

There was true *shalom* in the Garden of Eden before Adam and Eve disobeyed the LORD's one restriction. In yielding to Satan's deception and the enticement of becoming "like God, knowing good and evil," they yielded their high calling as rulers of creation under the LORD to Satan, who remains to this day "the prince of the powers of the air" (Ephesians 2:2). The whole of history as recorded in Scripture is God's unfolding plan to redeem, or buy back, mankind and finally restore shalom in the full sense to His creation.

Though we continue to live in a broken world, once we humble ourselves to admit our desperate need and trust Jesus as Savior, the Holy Spirit takes up residence in our inner self and we taste of His wonderful shalom.

Jesus stated, "Peace I leave with you; My peace I give to you. Not as the world gives do I give to you. Let not your hearts be troubled, neither let them be afraid.'" (John 14:27)

These flowers, representing God's incredibly varied and beautiful creation, are attached to a circle: the non-ending shape that could stand for eternity. One day the LORD will create a new heaven and a new earth where full, unlimited SHALOM will be enjoyed.

You are the light of the world. A city set on a hill cannot be hidden. Nor do people light a lamp and put it under a basket, but on a stand, and it gives light to all in the house. In the same way, let your light shine before others, so that they may see your good works and give glory to your Father Who is in heaven.

Matthew 5:14-16

So many of God's creatures move in community, in sync with one another; like schools of fish, flocks of geese, herds of sheep or deer, swarms of bees, colonies of ants. How about us?

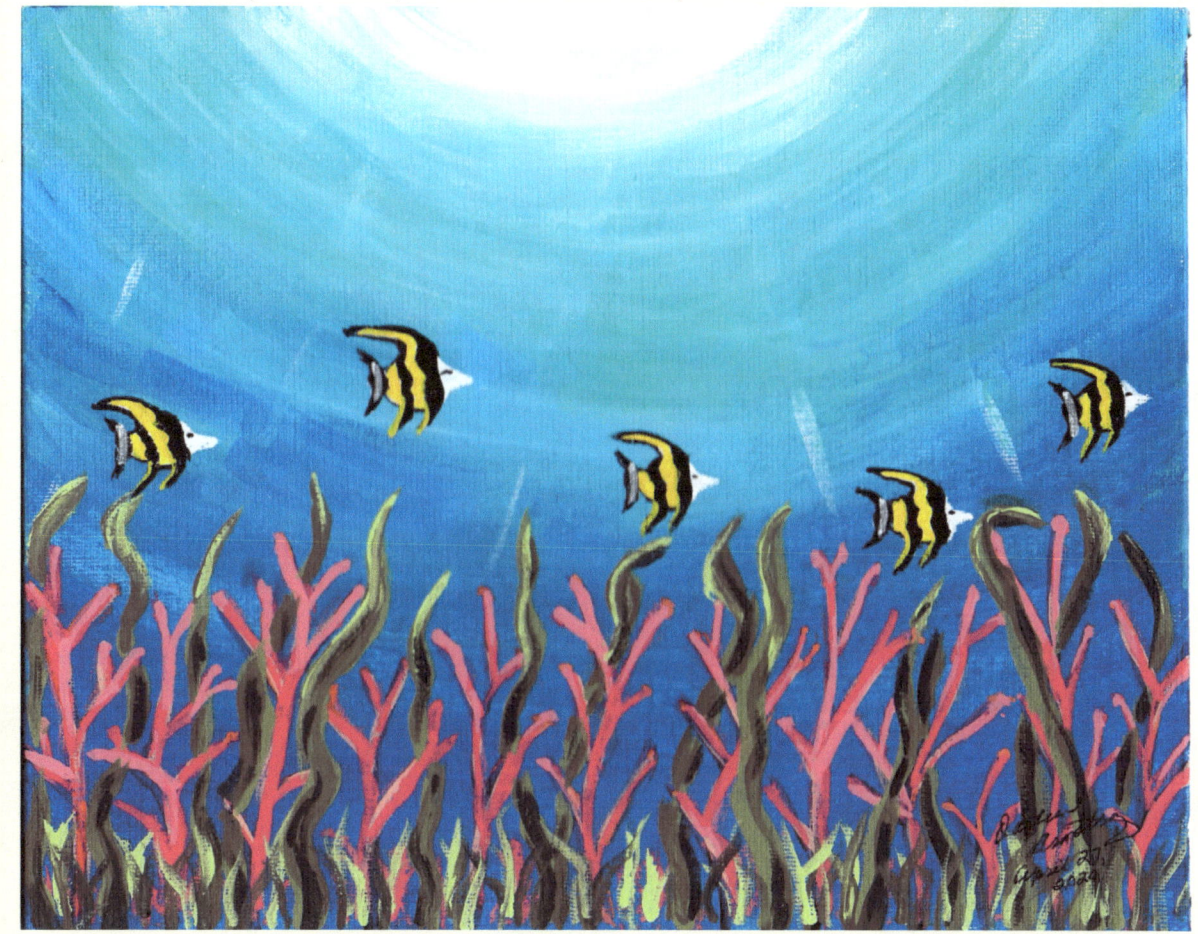

"So God created man in His own image, in the image of God He created him; male and female He created them." (Genesis 1:27) We were created for relationship, first and foremost with God. Before the Fall, Adam and Eve enjoyed fellowship with the LORD in the cool of the day, in full unity with each other. Rebellion of sin broke the relationship with God, which also broke the harmony with one another. It didn't take long after the sin curse of Genesis 3 for the first man child, Cain, to let jealousy move him to kill his brother Abel. How devastating that must have been for their parents: Adam and Eve! Thus began ongoing conflicts between individuals, groups and nations with little let up throughout history.

But God had a plan. He held the promise of restoration coming through His promised Messiah. Finally, in the fullness of time, God Almighty became man in the person of Jesus Christ. He came to redeem mankind to Himself. Through trusting in Jesus' death and resurrection we become reconciled with Holy God.

As His Spirit takes up residence in our heart of hearts, we begin seeing others through His eyes of love. I remember shortly after I admitted my need for a Savior and asked Jesus to make me His own as a young adult, how His understanding and compassion began to replace the belittling attitudes I had held toward some acquaintances. The Lord continues checking my attitudes towards others.

The New Testament contains numerous exhortations to love and respect one another. We do need national policies and laws to protect and help those who are being overlooked or taken advantage of. But real change in any culture happens when the Holy Spirit convicts and brings large numbers of individuals to repentance, faith in Christ and the transformation that follows. Let us continue to plead for a fresh work of God across our hurting nation.

"And no longer shall each one teach his neighbor and each his brother, saying, 'Know the Lord,' for they shall all know Me, from the least of them to the greatest, declares the Lord. For I will forgive their iniquity and I will remember their sin no more."

Thus says the Lord,

Who gives the sun for light by day

and the fixed order of the moon and the stars for light by night,

Who stirs up the sea so that its waves roar—

the Lord of hosts is His name:

Jeremiah 31:34, 35

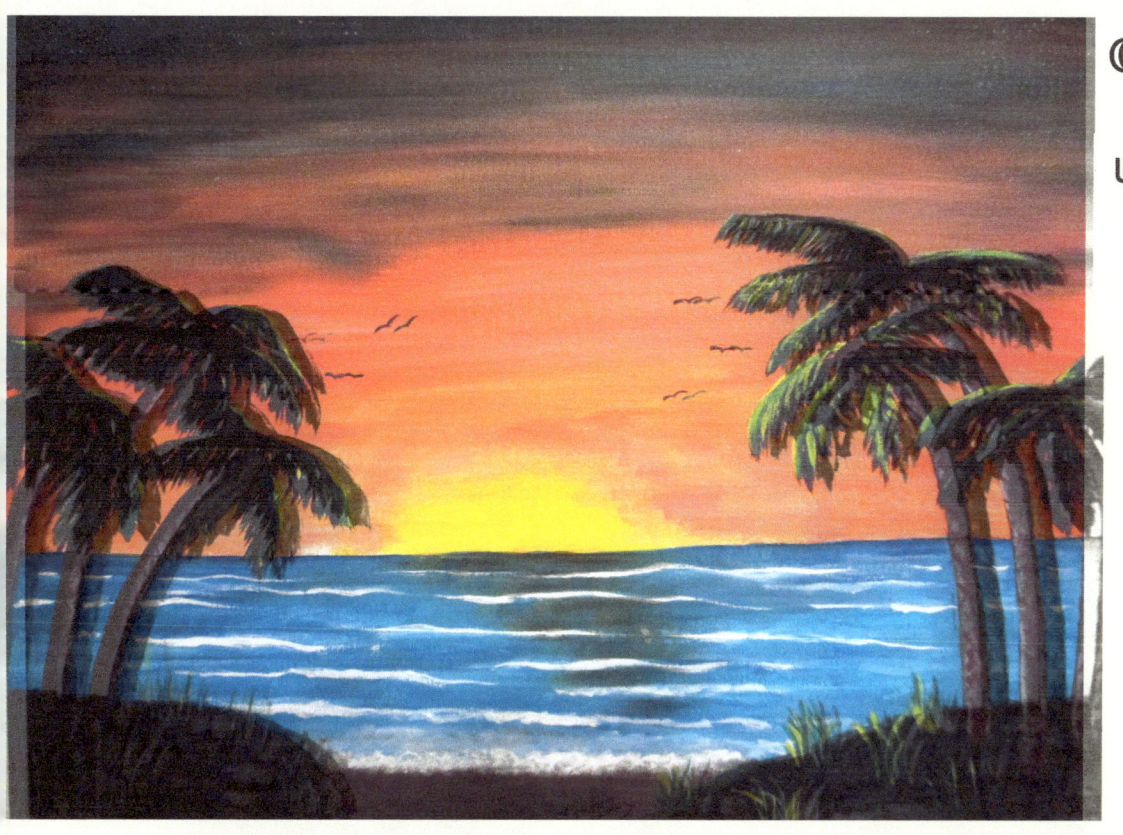

God's artwork is constantly painted across skies all around the globe, providing unique views from every possible position and continually changing. This tropical sunset reminds me of evenings in the Philippines when I served with SEND International in the late 1970's.

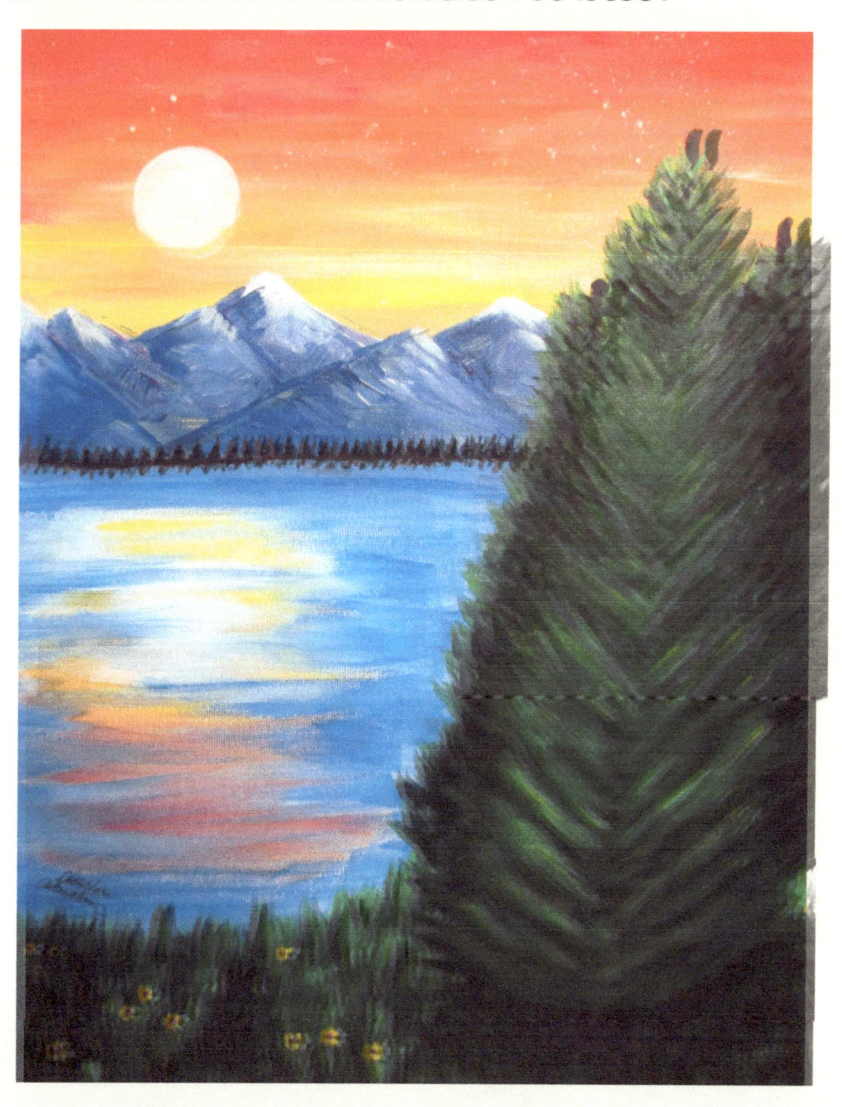

At the same time, a hiker may view the moon over a mountain lake. The same sun and moon shed light on people in contrasting environments and circumstances around this globe. It's good to know and ponder the fact that God knows intimately and cares deeply for every person on this earth!

A 17th Century hymn by Isaac Watts comes to mind,

"Jesus shall reign where'er the sun does His successive journeys run; His kingdom spread from shore to shore, till moons shall wax and wane no more."

Look at the birds of the air: they neither sow nor reap nor gather into barns, and yet your heavenly Father feeds them. Are you not of more value than they? And which of you by being anxious can add a single hour to his span of life?

-Jesus in Matthew 6:26-27

Despite the troubles of this world, the birds continue singing their melodious praises to their Creator. My dear friend, Diane, deals with harsh, chronic pain on top of leukemia that is active again, despite enduring 7 rounds of chemo through the years. We've both been touched by Joni Eareckson Tada's book, "A Place of Healing, Wrestling with the Mysteries of Suffering, Pain and God's Sovereignty."

Joni, quadriplegic since a diving accident at 17, was also experiencing severe, ongoing pain as she wrote. When everything seems overwhelming and the future looks bleak, she suggested I Thessalonians 5:16-18 as a place to start to gain a needed change of perspective. "Paul's succinct counsel will serve you very well no matter what your situation might be. Be joyful always. Pray continually. Give thanks in all circumstances." (p.164)

Later in that chapter she shared the power of a song. Joni sings praises from the time she awakens in the morning through all the routines of each day. She pointed out that the one time that the Bible records Jesus singing was with His disciples following the Last Supper, on His way to the Garden of Gethsemane, knowing that He soon faced crucifixion! (Matthew 26:30)

"So my friend, no matter if your emotions are up or down, follow the Lord's lead today. May the mind of Christ your Savior live in you from day to day, and ask God to simply put a song in your heart as you pick up your cross daily and follow Him. Singing is a perspective changer." (Joni, "A Place of Healing" p.180)

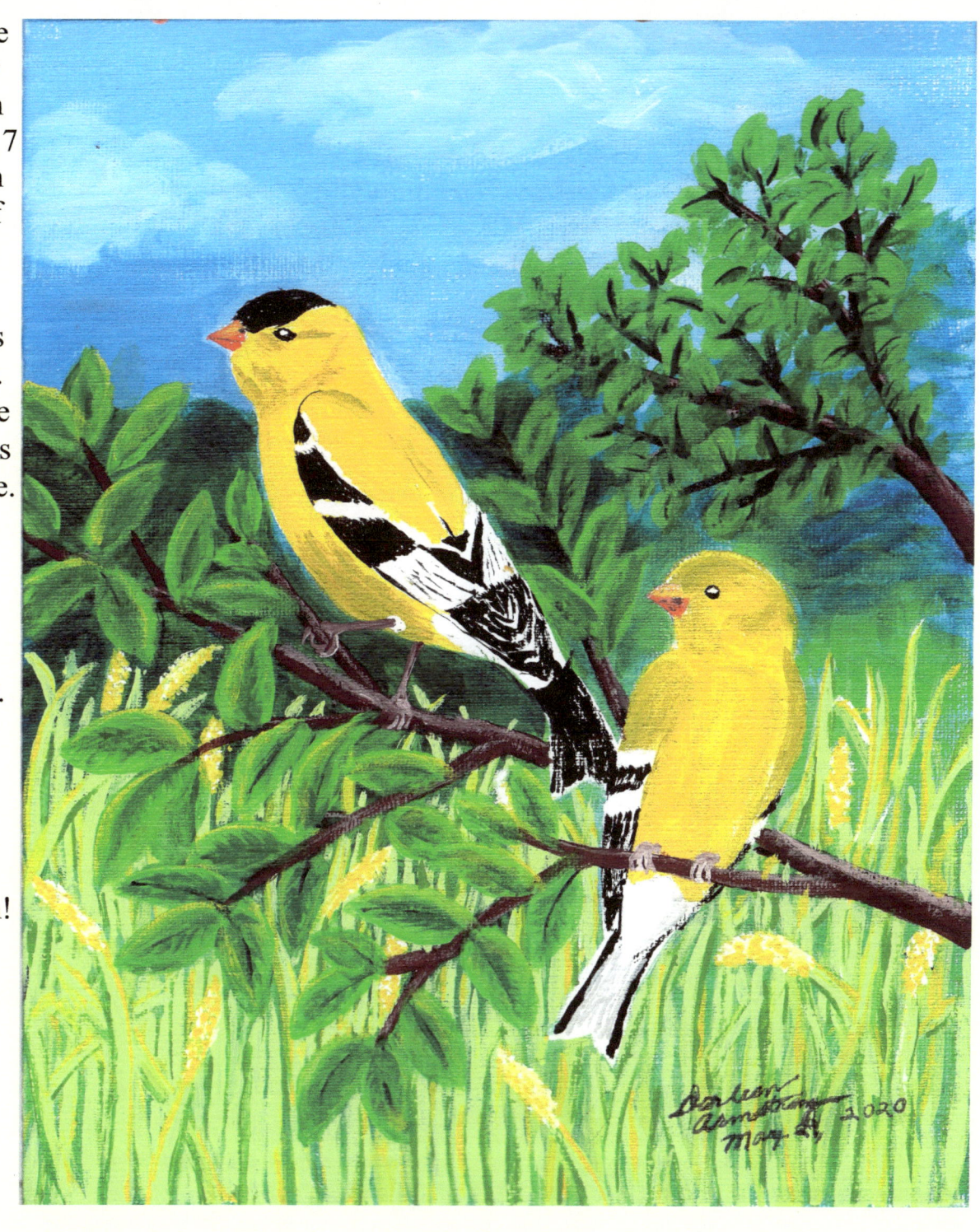

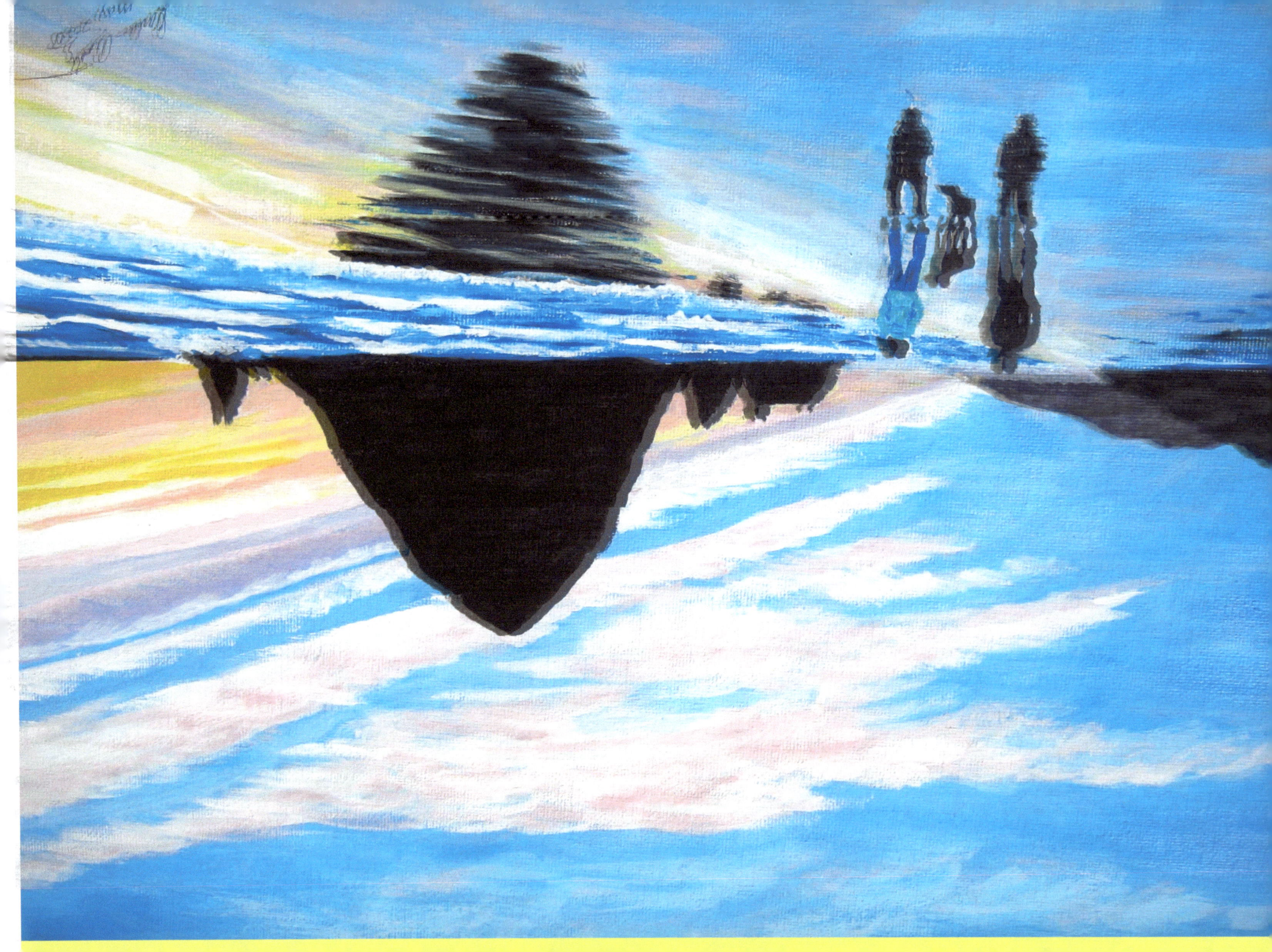

The ocean beach is one of my favorite places. When I found a photo I liked of Cannon Beach, I decided to try and capture it on canvas. As this pandemic wore on, I was longing to be there, longing for the sun to set, longing for an end to our restrictions. And the longing went further, for the end of the disruption, divisiveness, rage and violence across the cities of our nation. Reading recently through the books of Samuel and Kings and Chronicles, I noticed a repeated pattern. Again and again when God-fearing kings faced a major threat, they humbled themselves, acknowledged God's greatness and sovereignty, confessed the sins of their people and begged for God's help. Significantly, the LORD always answered positively.

"O our God, will you not execute judgment on them? For we are powerless against this great horde that is coming against us. We do not know what to do, but our eyes are on You." (2 Chronicles 20:12)

God responded to Jehoshaphat, giving instruction of what they were to do while the LORD did what only He could do. It is time for us to intercede like he did as we face major crises in America. The prayer for our nation that Anne Graham Lotz posted May 31, 2020, has been a helpful model. Here's a partial quote:

"Turn to us! Draw near to us! If You do not help us, we will be defenseless. If You do not protect us, we will be exposed to danger. If You do not deliver us from evil, we will be overcome by it. If You do not have plans to give us hope and a future, we will slide into the past tense as a nation. Into oblivion. We feel our nation sliding down even now...."

"Prince of Peace, breathe the cool, soothing wind of Your Spirit across the fiery rhetoric, rage, and rioting that have erupted. Grant us courage to face legitimate issues of injustice, oppression, and prejudice. Grant us the strength of character to set things right, while rejecting that which is wrong. Forgive us our sins as we forgive everyone who has sinned against us. Grant us Your peace...We ask that once again You would pour out Your Spirit on all flesh. Pour out Your blessings upon us.'"

Seek the Lord while He may be found;
call upon Him while He is near;
let the wicked forsake his way,
and the unrighteous man his thoughts;
let him return to the Lord, that He may
have compassion on him,
and to our God, for He will abundantly pardon.
For My thoughts are not your thoughts,
neither are your ways My ways, declares the Lord.
For as the heavens are higher than the earth,
so are My ways higher than your ways
and My thoughts than your thoughts.

Isaiah 55:6-9

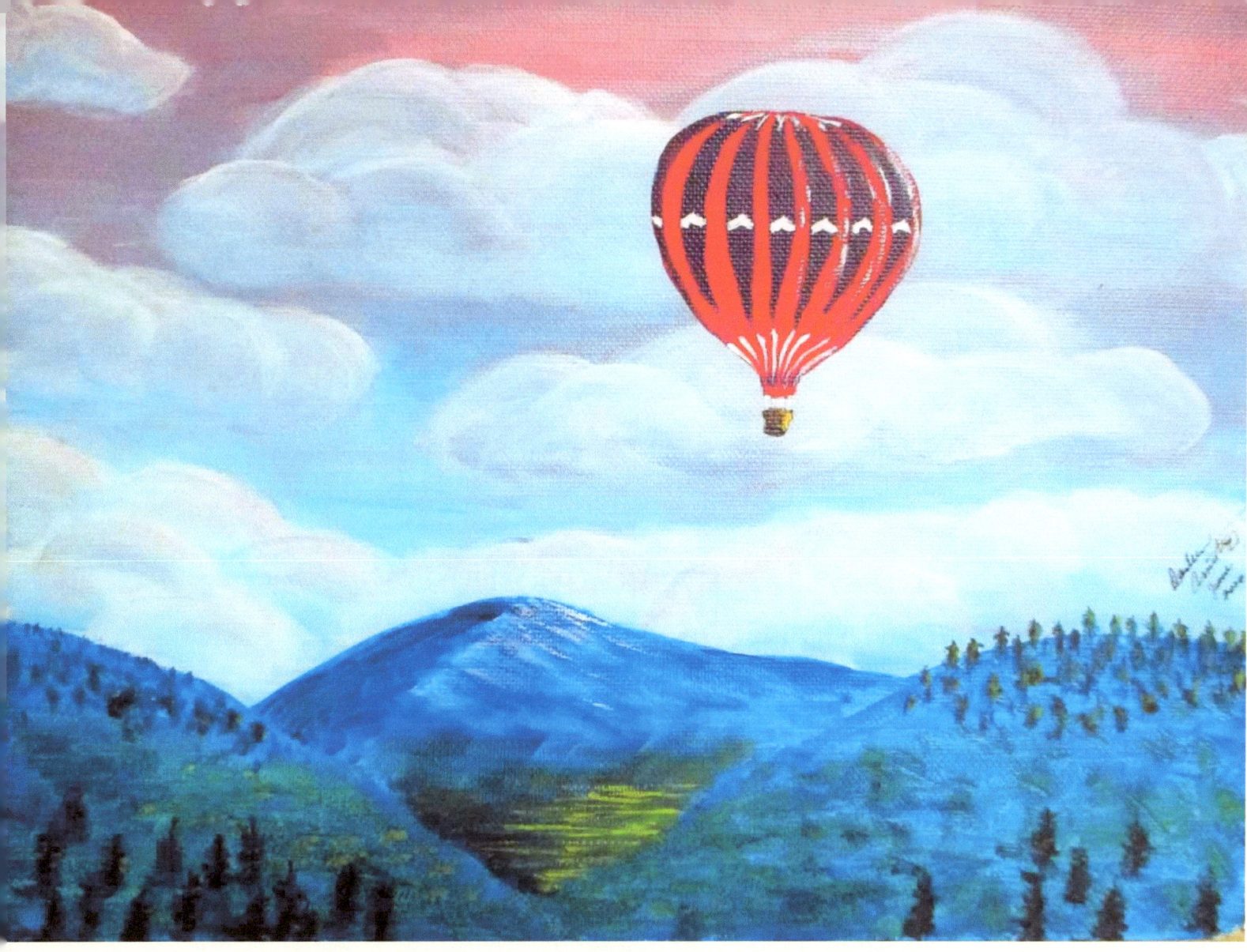

A hot air balloon was one of the last paintings that Debi demonstrated for us over the Internet during this pandemic. How lovely to think of rising and floating peacefully over the landscape. But my daughters reminded me, from watching a demonstration on *Reading Rainbow* some years back, that it's not very peaceful in that basket as the noisy blowers lift the balloon. The passengers could hardly hear each other when shouting!

Still, I imagine that once you had gained enough height, you could peacefully float just below the clouds. It would give you a much different perspective of the homes, busy highways and fields below. How needy we are of God's true perspective on life here! May we be lifted daily above our limited understanding of circumstances through His Word and His Spirit.

The One who sees the end from the beginning, has the true panoramic view of life.
I'm reminded of God's invitation to His prophet, Jeremiah

"Thus says the LORD who made the earth, the LORD Who formed it to establish it—the LORD is His Name: Call to Me and I will answer you, and will tell you great and hidden things that you have not known." (Jeremiah 33:2-3)

The people who walked in darkness
have seen a great LIGHT;
those who dwelt in a land of deep darkness,
on them has LIGHT shone.

Isaiah 9:2

We will all experience difficulties and trouble of various kinds. Our lives, like ships at sea, may enjoy days of relative peace and calm, but at other times the darkness and storms will threaten. Jesus and His Word are like our lighthouse. Whatever troubles may rage, we can cling to His promises.

But beyond this, Jesus promised never to leave or forsake His own. We can be assured of His very presence, right in our boat, as it were, with us. He knows, He cares, He is in charge with unlimited power. We have His promise,

"And we know that for those who love God all things work together for good, for those who are called according to His purpose." (Romans 8:28)

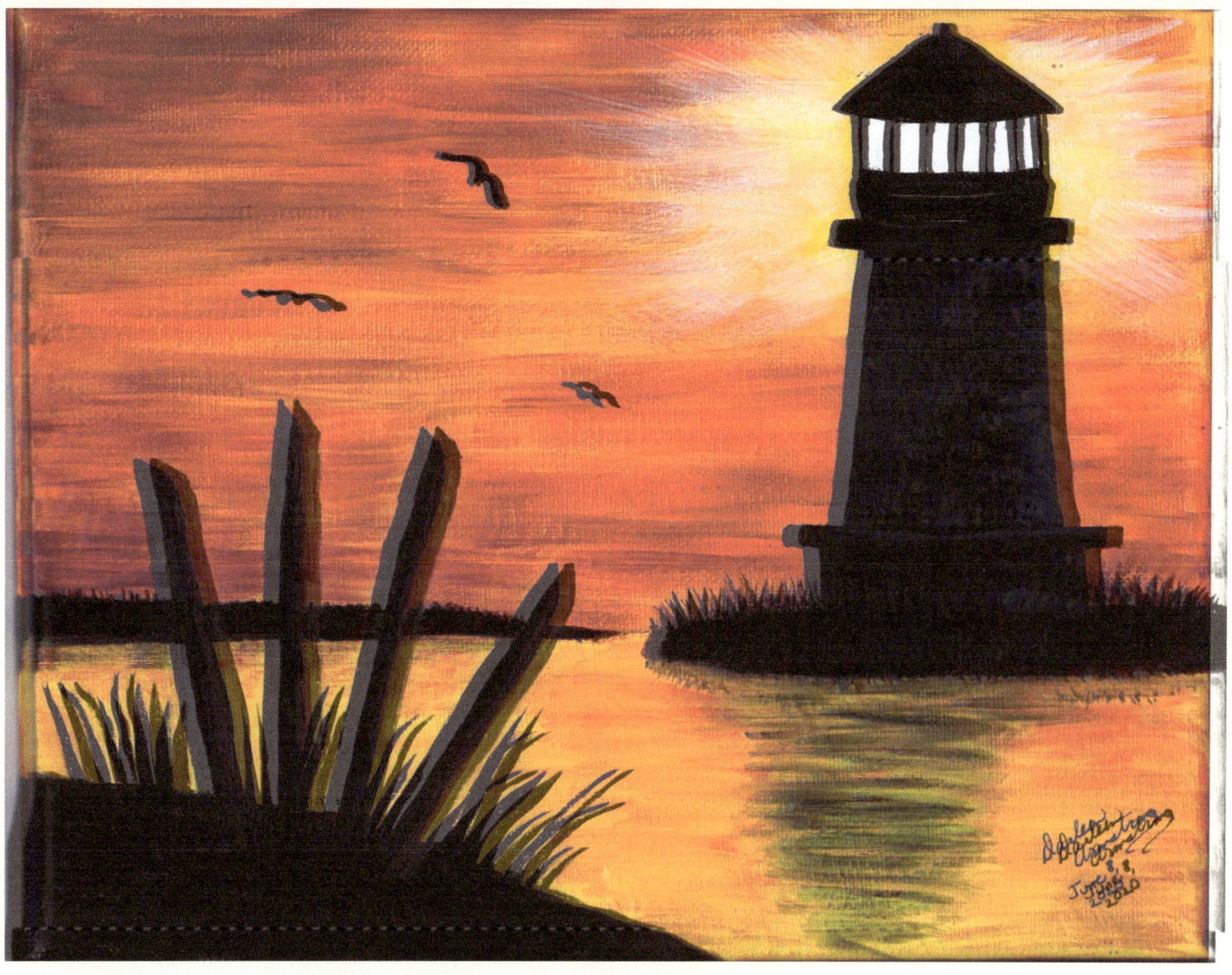

In fact, we also can find help and encouragement
as His light and love are expressed through others around us.

Thank You Lord Jesus that even during this COVID-19 pandemic and the racial tensions and rioting that distress our nation, there are individuals expressing your sacrificial and forgiving love, helping and sacrificing for others, preaching and teaching Gospel hope over the internet and calling many home to Yourself.
"The light shines in the darkness, and the darkness has not overcome it." (John 1:5)

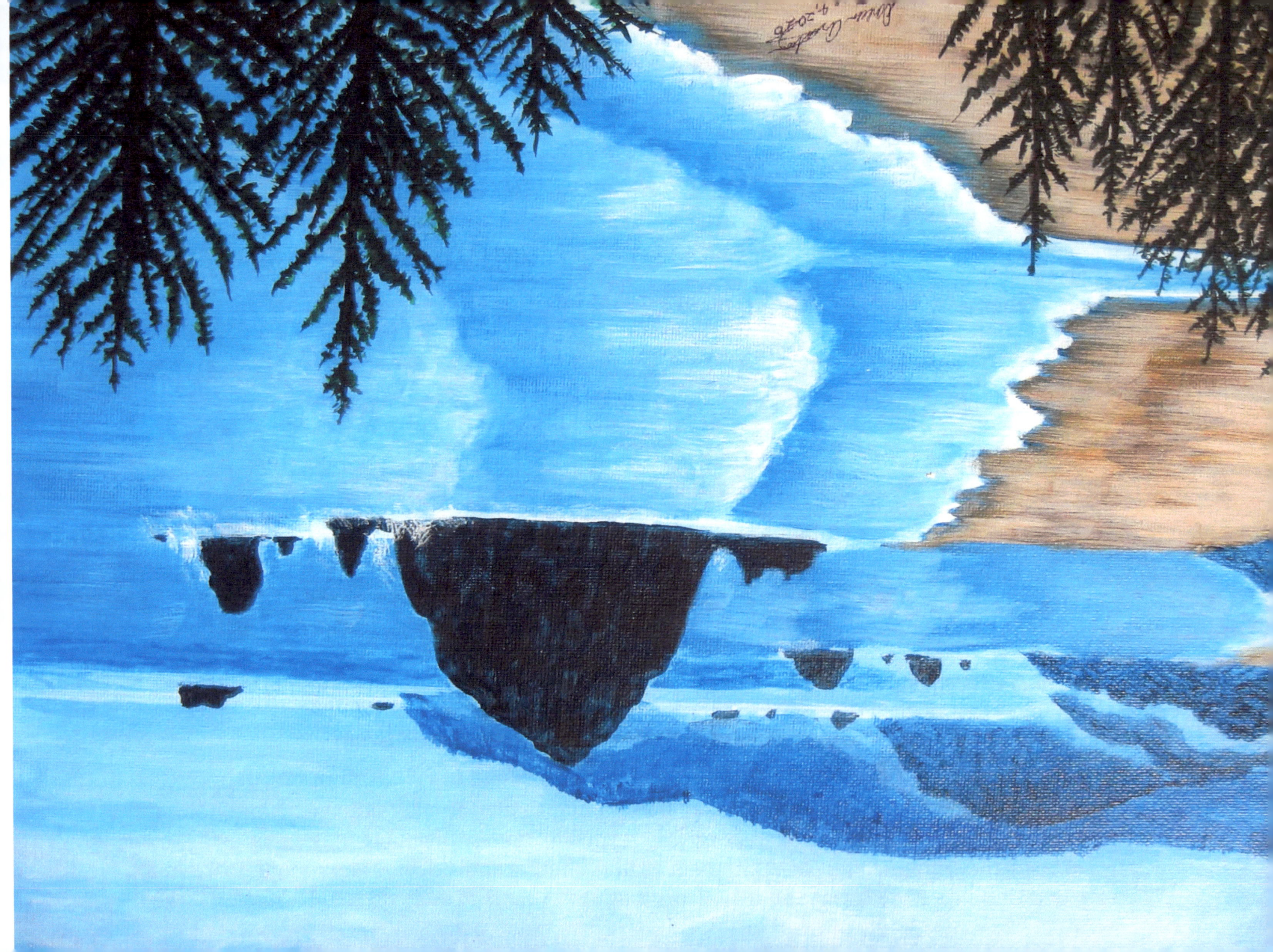

I close these ponderings with another painting that I tried on my own, using a photo as a model. Here's a different view of Canon Beach, one of the closest Oregon beaches for us, driving almost due west from our home. This time we look down from shady Ecola Park. This view touched my heart with memories and longing. The ocean makes me acutely aware of God's sovereign, mighty control. The prominent Haystack Rock, along with other protruding boulders, stands against the mighty waves, providing refuge to many sea birds and housing other creatures who cling to the sturdy sides and are fed by the waves.

How I love to walk along the seashore, hearing the rhythmic sound of waves and surf mingled with squawking sea gulls. I enjoy feeling the warmth of the sun mixed with salty breezes. It's fun to scan the broken pits of shells on the shore, searching for that rare, whole specimen. And then there are the tide pools with their miniature aquarium worlds of sea anemones, starfish, barnacles, crabs and tiny fish.

And I'll gaze out at the blue horizon, wondering what sea creatures swim just below the surface? There's a lively, teeming world in the depths below those waves!

"Or who shut in the sea with doors when it burst out from the womb, when I made clouds its garment and thick darkness its swaddling band, and prescribed limits for it and set bars and doors, and said 'Thus far shall you come, and no farther, and here shall your proud waves be stayed'?" (Job 38:8-11)

Let us praise our great God and Savior, Who created and sustains the universe and all it contains . There are many Psalms, hymns and songs that could assist us. Recently, I've been using the wonderful declaration of praise for our Savior and Lord penned by Paul in the first chapter of Colossians. I like to change the pronouns to first person to speak this directly to Christ Jesus:

"You are the image of the invisible God, the firstborn of all creation. For by You all things were created, in heaven and on earth, visible and invisible, whether thrones or dominions or rulers or authorities all things were created through You and for You. And You are before all things, and in You all things hold together. And You are the head of the body, the church. You are the beginning, the firstborn from the dead, that in everything You might be preeminent. For in You all the fullness of God was pleased to dwell, and through You to reconcile to Himself all things, whether on earth or in heaven, making peace by the blood of Your cross." (Colossians 1:15-20)

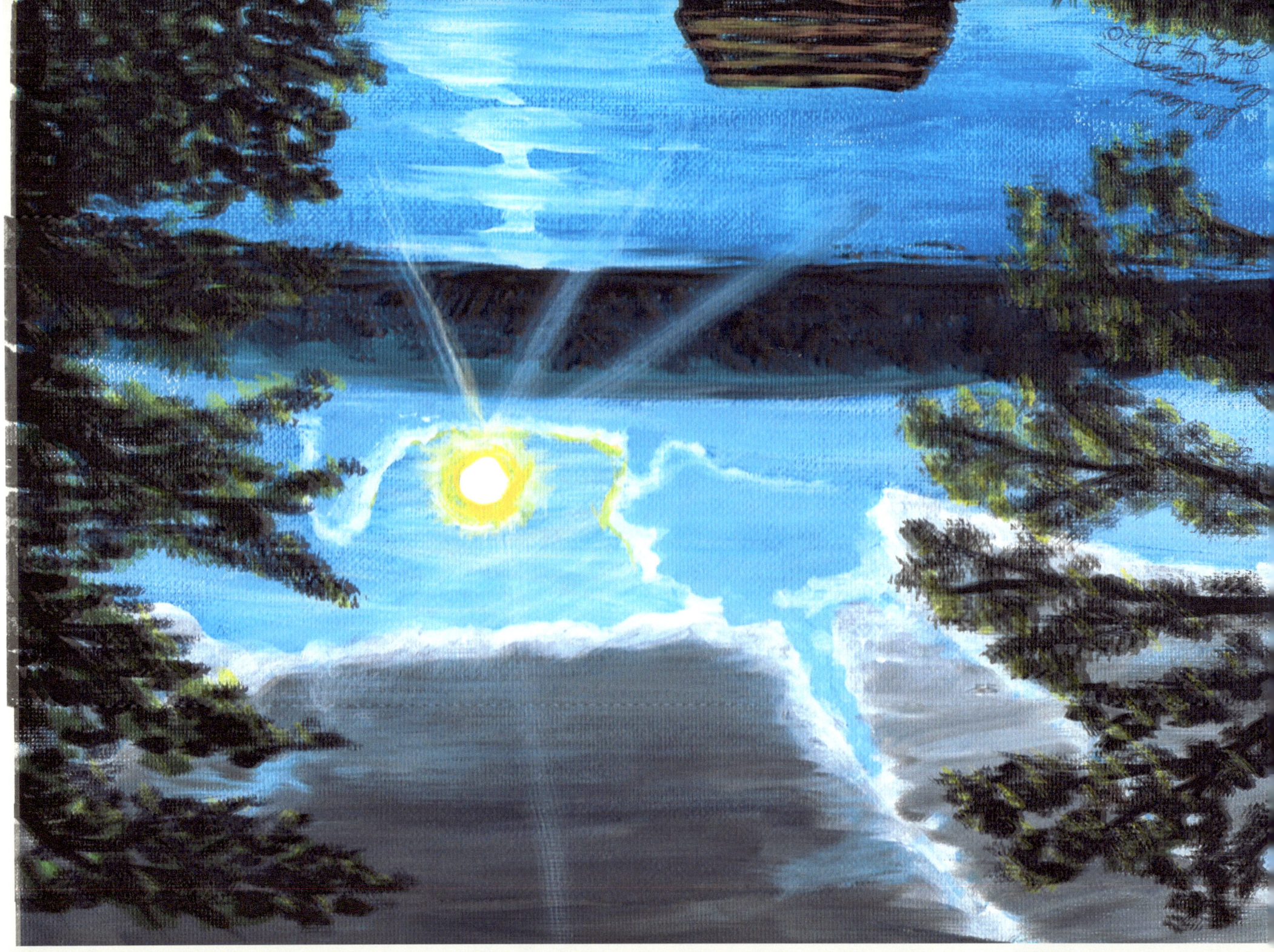

Here's one additional painting finished on a quiet Fourth of July afternoon (before our neighborhood erupted with fireworks). It was inspired by a dramatic photo my niece, Kristen, posted on Facebook of storm clouds over Lake Henry. It's like the bright sun is reminding us, "although clouds and storms will block my light, know that I'll still be here, shining just beyond the clouds."

The Apostle John wrote late in his life, "This is the message we have heard from Him and proclaim to you, that God is light, and in Him is no darkness at all." (1 John 1:5)

How wonderful that we can approach and be welcomed into God's holy light through trusting in Jesus's redemptive death and resurrection!

"See what kind of love the Father has given to us, that we should be called children of God; and so we are. The reason why the world does not know us is that it did not know Him. Beloved, we are God's children now, and what we will be has not yet appeared;
but we know that when he appears we shall be like Him, because we shall see Him as He is." (1 John 3:1-2)

May we live each day in light of that expectation!

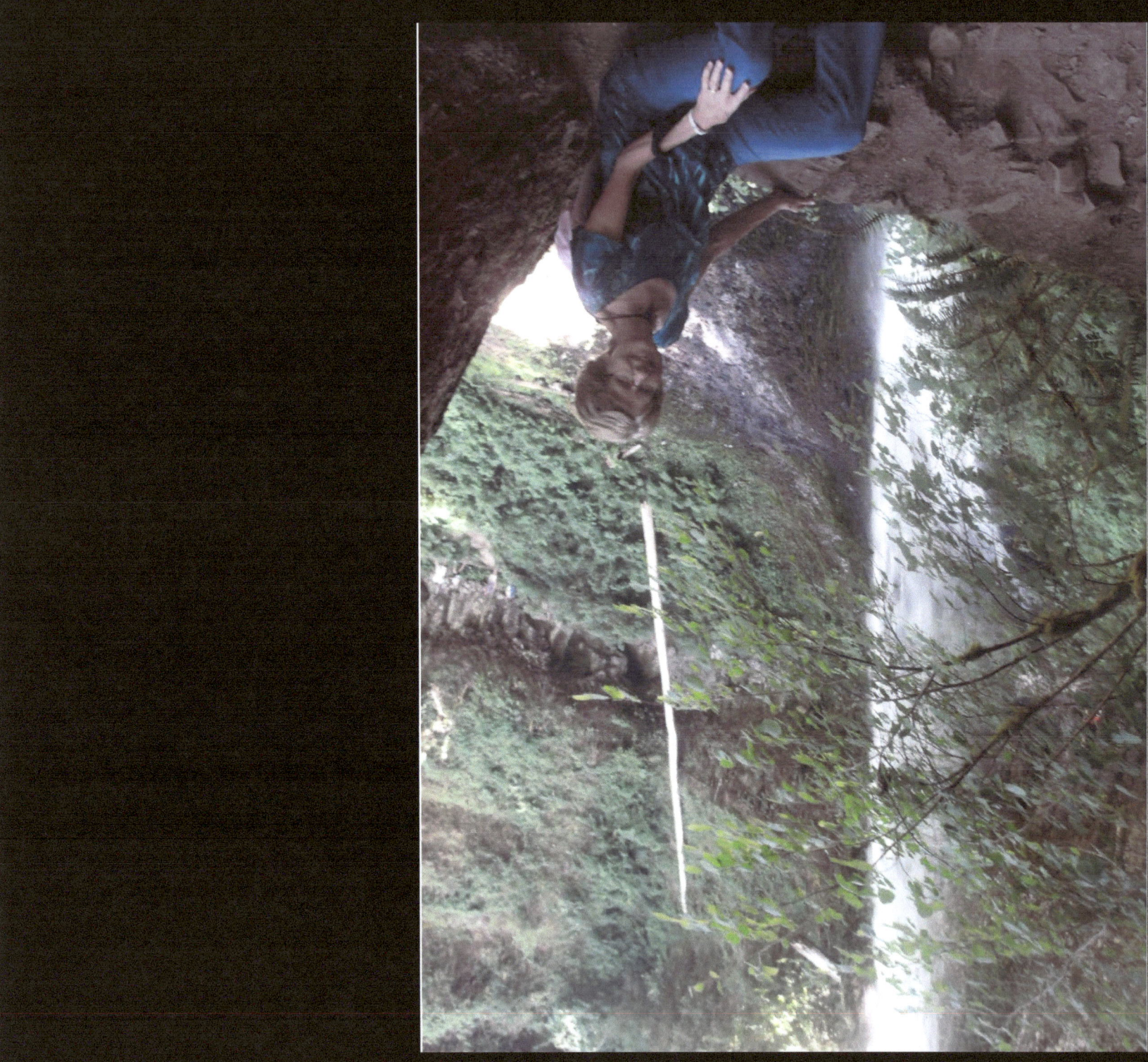

Thank you for joining me in this journey of art and faith. It is my prayer that you, dear reader are reminded of the Living Hope in Jesus!

    I knew about God for many years while directing my own life before I realized that I actually needed to yield my life to Him. We were created for relationship with God, but in the natural, we are separated from Him, rebels in our self-sufficiency and pride. Jesus bridged the huge gap when He, fully God, became man to become our substitute. As the only perfect, sinless man, He took God's wrath for sin on Himself on the cross, then rose victorious from death. "but God shows His love for us in that while we were still sinners, Christ died for us." (Romans 5:8) The moment I repented of trusting in myself and asked Jesus to enter my life, He did! I've known His love and presence ever since. And He continues His transforming work from the inside out.

    Have you come to know Christ personally yet, dear reader? He loves you more than you can imagine. In this difficult world, Jesus is the source of true lasting hope, unconditional love, and perfect eternal life to come for all who trust in Him. I hope to share God's glorious heaven with you one day!

    -Darleen